The Jacket

BY **ANDREW CLEMENTS**

ILLUSTRATED BY

MCDAVID HENDERSON

HAMPTON-BROWN

THE EXCHANGE

What can make people misunderstand each other?

THANKS TO RAY SHEPARD FOR HIS
FRIENDSHIP, GENEROSITY, AND CANDOR.
I THANK LUCILLE TATE, LONG DEPARTED NOW,
FOR HER SWEETNESS AND TOLERANCE.

—A.C.

Hampton-Brown
P.O. Box 223220
Carmel, California 93922
800-333-3510
www.hampton-brown.com

Printed in the United States of America

ISBN-13: 978-0-7362-2792-6
ISBN-10: 0-7362-2792-X

06 07 08 09 10 11 12 13 14 10 9 8 7 6 5 4 3 2

The Jacket

Phil needs to find his brother Jimmy at school.
He sees another boy wearing Jimmy's jacket.
He thinks that the boy stole the jacket. Both boys
go to the principal's office.

Part I

COLLISION COURSE

It was Thursday morning right before first period, and Phil **was on a mission**. Hurrying through the fourth- and fifth-grade hall, he **waded** through groups of younger kids. His little brother, Jimmy, had left the house early so he could ride to school with a friend, and he had forgotten his lunch money on the kitchen counter.

Phil was tall for a sixth grader, so most of the younger kids **got out of his way**. Which was good, because he had no time to **mess around**. If he got one more tardy during December, he would have

....

was on a mission had a job to do
waded walked with difficulty
got out of his way moved so they were not in his way
mess around do things that were not important

to serve two detentions. The pressure made **Phil's imagination run at full throttle**. *Like, if I'm late for math today, then I might not be allowed to take the test—and then I could flunk math! I might even flunk sixth grade and get left back! And when Mom and Dad yell at me, I'm gonna get so mad, 'cause, like, it's not even my fault! I'll say, "Hey, know what? Forget about school, that's what!" And I'll just drop out and turn into a bum—or maybe even a criminal. My whole life's gonna be a mess, and it's all on account of my stupid little brother! Where is that punk?*

Phil was about to stick his head into a classroom to look around. Then up at the corner of the hallway he thought he saw the back of his brother's jacket. It had to be Jimmy. No one else in the whole city had a jacket like that one.

He called, "Hey, Jimmy!" but his brother didn't stop, and Phil pushed his way forward and rushed around the corner. "Hey, idiot, you forgot . . . "

But it wasn't Jimmy. It was someone Phil had never seen before, a black kid. Wearing Jimmy's jacket.

....

Phil's imagination run at full throttle Phil think about
everything at one time

Phil grabbed the collar and said, "Hey! This is my brother's jacket! Where is he? How'd you get this from him?"

The other boy struggled, trying to pull away. "What're you talkin' about? Let go of me! This is my jacket! I don't even know your brother!"

The kid twisted and turned to **break free**, but Phil was a lot bigger and stronger. "You tell me where my brother's at, or I'm gonna—"

"Boys! You stop it, right now!" Mrs. Atkin **came striding** through the crowd that had gathered, pushing kids out of her way with her left hand and pointing at Phil with the other one. "You let go of him, and I mean it!"

Drawn by Mrs. Atkin's voice, three or four other teachers stepped out into the hallway.

Phil let go of the jacket, and the younger boy jerked around to face him, his fists up, his eyes narrowed.

Mrs. Atkin stepped between them and said to the younger boy, "Daniel, you put your hands down.

---

break free get away
came striding walked in long steps
Drawn by When they heard

And all the rest of you kids, **go on about your business**. Get your things put away and get to your rooms. Go on, there's nothing happening here."
Then, **glaring** at Phil and the smaller boy, she said, "You two, come with me."

....

go on about your business return to what you were doing

glaring looking in an angry way

BEFORE YOU MOVE ON...

1. **Narrator's Point of View** Who tells the story? Look for pronouns on page 7 to help you.

2. **Inference** Reread page 10. What do you think Phil assumed about Daniel?

LOOK AHEAD Read pages 12–17 to find out why Daniel calls Phil a liar.

The other teachers were moving around in the hallway now, talking to kids, quieting everyone down.

Phil and Daniel followed Mrs. Atkin along the hall. And Phil knew where they were headed—straight to the office. He thought, *Now I'm gonna flunk out for sure.*

At the office door Mrs. Atkin stopped and **herded** the boys in ahead of her. "Mrs. Cormier? Sorry to start your day like this, but I found these two **going at it** down in the fourth-grade hall. I've got to get back to my room before something else **breaks loose**."

The principal still had her coat on from being out at the curb with the buses. She frowned at the boys and pointed toward her office. "Walk in and sit down. And I don't want you two to even *look* at each other, is that clear?"

Both of them nodded and walked into her office.

A minute later Mrs. Cormier came in and sat down behind her desk. She motioned to Phil, who

....

herded moved
going at it fighting
breaks loose happens

had taken a chair against the wall. "Come over here and sit in front of me. I want to be able to **look each of you in the eye**."

Daniel kept looking straight ahead at Mrs. Cormier. When Phil was seated, she said, "Phil, **you've got no business being** in the four-five hall in the morning. Why were you there?"

"My brother, Jimmy, forgot his lunch money. And I still have to give it to him."

Mrs. Cormier nodded. "All right, **that makes sense**. Here," she said, putting out her hand, "give me his money, and I'll make sure he gets it."

Phil dug in his pocket and gave the coins to the principal. She put them on her desk and then turned to the other boy. "Okay, Daniel, you first: What happened?"

"What happened is, I'm talking with my friends, and this kid comes and grabs me and starts yelling at me. I've never seen him before. I didn't do a thing!"

Mrs. Cormier turned to Phil. "Did you grab him, Phil?"

....

look each of you in the eye see each of your faces
you've got no business being there is no reason you should be
that makes sense I understand

"Yeah, 'cause he stole my brother's jacket! That's my old jacket, and now it's my brother's, and this kid stole it, so I grabbed him."

"Liar!" Daniel jumped to his feet and faced Phil, his fists **clenched**. "I never stole a thing! My gramma gave me this jacket for my birthday, and that's the truth, so you stop saying that!"

"Daniel," said Mrs. Cormier sharply, "you sit down and stay put!" Mrs. Cormier **swept her eyes between the boys**. "I think this is a simple **misunderstanding**. Phil, isn't it possible that Daniel happens to have a jacket just like your brother's?"

Phil shook his head forcefully. "No way. My mom bought that jacket when she went to Italy, and she brought it back for me. Go ahead, look at the label inside the neck. It's gonna say 'Ricci di Roma.' That's because she got it in Rome. Go ahead and look. That's my jacket."

Mrs. Cormier stood up and walked around to the front of her desk. "May I look at the label, Daniel?"

....

clenched pushed together tightly; squeezed

swept her eyes between the boys looked at one boy and then the other

misunderstanding mistake

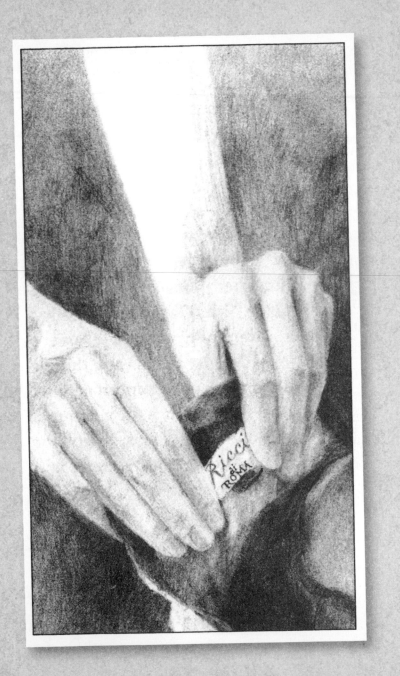

He shrugged and stuck his lower lip out. "I don't care. 'Cause this isn't his jacket."

The principal gently pulled the collar of the jacket back, and then **twisted her neck and adjusted her glasses**. **Her eyebrows shot up.** "It says 'Ricci di Roma.'"

"See? I told you so," said Phil **triumphantly**. "He stole it!"

....

twisted her neck and adjusted her glasses turned her neck and moved her glasses closer to her eyes

Her eyebrows shot up. She looked surprised.

triumphantly as if he had won

BEFORE YOU MOVE ON...

1. **Summarize** Reread pages 15–17. Daniel called Phil a liar because Phil said Daniel stole the jacket. What did Daniel say?

2. **Conclusions** Look at pages 15–16. How did Phil know the jacket belonged to his brother?

LOOK AHEAD Read to page 21 to find out why Phil apologizes to Daniel.

"Did not, you big liar!" And if Mrs. Cormier hadn't been on her feet to catch him, Daniel would have been on top of Phil, fists swinging. She pushed him back into his chair and shouted, "Silence! **Not another word**, either of you!" Calling to the secretary through the open door, she said, "Mrs. Donne? Get me the **emergency cards** for Philip Morelli and Daniel Taylor, would you—right away."

Thirty seconds later Mrs. Cormier was dialing her phone, then smiling and speaking. "Mrs. Taylor? This is Mrs. Cormier, the principal at Daniel's school. . . . No, he's fine, but there's been a disagreement this morning, and he's **in the middle of it**. It's about a jacket, the one Daniel says he got for his birthday. Another boy is here, and he says the jacket belongs to him. Can you tell me anything else that might help? . . . Yes. . . . Oh. I see. . . . So it was a gift. . . . Yes, I see. Well, that's it, then. I'm awfully sorry to have bothered you. . . . Yes, you too. Good-bye."

Daniel turned to Phil. "See? I told you so. It was

....

Not another word Do not say anything else
emergency cards cards with the phone numbers of the parents
in the middle of it an important part of it

a gift—for me."

Mrs. Cormier said, "It turns out you're both right, boys. Someone gave that jacket to your grandmother, Daniel, and then she gave it to you."

Phil made a face. "Gave it to his grandmother? How come?"

Mrs. Cormier started to say something, then stopped, smiled awkwardly, and said, "Well, really, I . . . I think it was just . . . to be kind. That's all."

Something **registered in Phil's mind**, and his mouth dropped open. Turning to Daniel, he asked, "Who's your grandma? What's her name?"

Daniel **curled his lip**. "**None of your business.** But her name's Lucy. Lucy Taylor."

Phil's face reddened. "Hey, look. I'm sorry I grabbed you, okay? You're right. It's your jacket."

"What?" Daniel looked sideways at Phil, **cocking** his head as if he hadn't heard clearly. "You come and almost pull this thing off my back, and now you say just keep it? What's that about?"

....

registered in Phil's mind made Phil think differently

curled his lip made an angry smile

None of your business. It is not something you need to know about.

cocking moving

Phil looked at the floor. "It's just that . . . like, I think I know your grandma—that's all. So the jacket's yours."

Daniel frowned and narrowed his eyes. "*You?* Know my gramma? Right!" He smiled, **taunting Phil**. "Yeah, like, how you gonna know my gramma? Maybe you see her when you go to the same beauty parlor she does, huh? That it?"

Mrs. Cormier stood up and said, "Boys, that's enough. **This is all settled.** Daniel, Phil said he's sorry, and we know the jacket is yours. So both of you run along to class now. Mrs. Donne will give you notes for your teachers."

Daniel stood up. He stuck his chin out and said, "Fine with me. Because this boy just keeps telling lies and lies. Like how he knows my gramma."

"I do too know her!" Phil almost shouted. "I'm not a liar! I see her all the time because . . . because she's my mom's cleaning lady!"

The words seemed to **echo** off the walls.

---

taunting Phil saying things in a way that would make Phil angry
This is all settled. This fight is now over.
echo bounce

Daniel looked like he'd been punched in the stomach. He backed toward the office door, his face **working angrily**. He **yanked the jacket open, pulled himself free of it**, and threw it on the floor at Phil's feet. "There's your jacket! You take it and you tell yo' momma that my gramma and me don't need nobody being *kind* to us!" And looking at Mrs. Cormier, he snarled, *"Nobody!"*

....

working angrily looking angry
yanked the jacket open, pulled himself free of it quickly opened the jacket, and took it off

BEFORE YOU MOVE ON...

1. **Sequence** Phil apologized when he found out the jacket was Daniel's. How did the jacket get from Italy to Daniel?

2. **Inference** Reread pages 20–21. Why do you think Daniel threw the jacket on the floor?

LOOK AHEAD Read to page 26 to find out what Phil learns about friendship.

Phil thinks about Daniel and the jacket. He remembers how upset Daniel was. Daniel shows Phil how it feels to be embarrassed. Phil notices Daniel is not wearing a jacket.

Part II

FRIENDS WITH EVERYBODY

The rest of Phil's Thursday wasn't so good. Compared with the **thoughts swirling through his mind**, decimals and adjectives and Ancient Egypt didn't seem very important.

Phil knew that all he had done was tell the truth. About the lunch money, about the jacket, about Daniel's grandmother. It was all true. But

---

thoughts swirling through his mind many things he was thinking about he couldn't **shake the feeling** that he'd done something bad.

He kept thinking about the early morning scene in the principal's office, replaying it again and again. He kept seeing the look on Daniel's face, the anger in his eyes as he threw the jacket to the floor. And **instinctively** Phil knew that **his being white and Daniel's being black was part of this**. Maybe a big part.

Phil had known a lot of African American kids at school, ever since his first day as a kindergartner. And he thought, *I don't care what color anybody is. I never pay attention to that. I'm friends with everybody.*

But being friends with everyone and being someone's friend, those were two different things. And as he thought about it, Phil knew he had never had a black kid for a friend, not really. The kids on the school basketball team were good guys, but not really friends. Black kids went to his school, but did they live in his neighborhood? Not in his part of the city. That's just how things were. Every morning

---

shake the feeling stop thinking

instinctively with no need to think about it

his being white and Daniel's being black was part of this
part of the problem was that Phil was white and Daniel was black

Daniel and the other African American kids arrived at school by bus, or sometimes their parents dropped them off. A lot of Hispanic kids, too. Phil didn't know exactly where they came from. It didn't really matter to him, and he'd never thought about it much. Until today.

Phil kept **arguing with himself**. He thought, *Yeah, but during school, everyone **gets along fine**— white kids, Hispanic kids, Asian kids, black kids. No problems.*

Most of the African American kids sat together at lunch, and they **tended to hang around** together in the halls and at recess. But that didn't seem weird to Phil. When you eat lunch, or if you have a little free time, you want to be with your friends, that's all. Besides, everyone played sports together during gym, and sometimes at recess, too. Everyone, together. No problems. *And all the black guys on my basketball team? I get along great with them.*

Still, after school every day almost all the black

----

arguing with himself thinking hard about it
gets along fine is friends
tended to hang around usually would stand and talk

kids got onto buses or climbed into cars and drove away. Those kids just **disappeared** as Phil went to basketball practice or walked home with his friends.

---

disappeared left; went a different way

BEFORE YOU MOVE ON...

1. **Conclusions** Phil learned "being friends with everyone" was different from "being someone's friend." What did he mean?

2. **Conflict** Was the problem between Phil and Daniel more than who owned the jacket? Why?

LOOK AHEAD Phil thinks he knows Daniel's grandmother very well. Read pages 27–31 to find out why.

Sitting in math class, Phil thought about Daniel's grandmother. *I've known her longer than Daniel has!* And it was true. He was two years older than Daniel, and Phil had known Lucy **all his life**.

Lucy. That's what he'd always called her. Just Lucy. She came every other Saturday and helped his mom clean the house. Phil had never even wondered about her last name. It had never mattered. She was just Lucy. Until today.

When he was little, Phil had loved helping on cleaning day. He would take hold of the bucket with all the supplies in it and **heave** it up the front stairs, one at a time. Lucy would smile and say, "Why, Philip, look at you! You sure are big and strong!"

And now that he was almost twelve, sometimes as he ran through the house to get a baseball glove or **grab a quick bite of lunch** before going out to shoot baskets with his friends, Lucy would look up from her work and narrow her eyes at him. She'd put her hands on her hips and say, "Isn't that **just the way**—now you're big enough to really help your

---

all his life since he was born

heave carry

grab a quick bite of lunch eat lunch quickly

just the way how it always happens

mama, and do you? No, 'cause you've got too much goin' on to be bothered with that!"

But that was just to tease him. Because it wasn't like Phil didn't do chores. He did plenty around the house. He took out the trash, raked the yard, mowed the grass, shoveled snow in the winter—stuff like that.

And he didn't mind doing housework, either. But Mom always said he and Jimmy didn't do it right. She said, "You guys pick up the big pieces, things like shoes and dirty clothes. Leave the little stuff for me and Lucy to worry about." Which was fine with him.

Phil kept trying to **reason away his feelings**. *Can I help it* if we have a cleaning lady, and she's black and we're white? And can I help it if she's Daniel's grandmother? I mean, it's not like we're rich or something. It's not like we force Lucy to work for us, is it?

Which was true, especially about not being rich. His mom and dad each had a full-time job. And back when Phil was born, his mom had decided to give herself a **treat** once every two weeks—that's

....

reason away his feelings think of why he should not feel bad

Can I help it Is it my fault

treat present, reward

what she called it, a treat. And that was having Lucy come to help her do the **deep cleaning**.

Phil thought about his own grandmothers. He had two, one here in the city and one in Florida. His mother's mom was the one who lived close. Grandma Morcone was sort of rich. She and Grandpa lived in **a condominium** on Herndon Street, not too far from the big museum. Her place was way up on the fourteenth floor. You could see the city parks from her windows, and the view looked like this beautiful painting. On the Fourth of July and sometimes on New Year's Eve, Phil and Jimmy and their big sister, Juliana, would sit with their grandparents on the balcony and watch the fireworks.

Grandma Morcone had long arms, thin and white. She wore silver bracelets on both wrists, and on one of her hands there was a ring with a big green stone in it. Phil could picture her fine clothes, her small diamond earrings, her silver blue hair, always neatly styled. His grandma didn't clean

---

deep cleaning difficult cleaning, like washing floors
a condominium an apartment that she owned

houses for other families. She probably never put a **bandanna over her hair** and pulled on yellow rubber gloves. Like Lucy did.

....

bandanna over her hair scarf on to keep the dust out of her hair

BEFORE YOU MOVE ON...

1. **Summarize** Phil has known Lucy all his life. Tell about Phil and Lucy's relationship.

2. **Comparisons** Reread pages 30–31. How were Lucy and Grandma Morcone different?

LOOK AHEAD Read pages 32–36 to see how Daniel embarrasses Phil.

At lunchtime Phil **edged** into the cafeteria. He **scanned** the big room, looking for Daniel. He wasn't there, and Phil was glad. He got in line and started loading food onto his tray—grilled cheese, red Jell-O, carrot sticks, chocolate milk, and an ice-cream sandwich.

The lady at the end of the counter took his money, looked at his tray, and then shook her head. "You need another quarter, honey. Or else put the ice cream back."

Phil dug deep into his pockets, but he didn't have another quarter. And he knew why. This morning when he gave the principal Jimmy's lunch money, he had given away too much.

Phil had picked up the ice cream from his tray when a voice behind him said, "That's okay. Here's another quarter." Phil smiled and turned to say "Thanks," but he stopped before the word came out.

It was Daniel. He was three kids back in the lunch line, and he was holding up a quarter, and he was smiling. But it wasn't a real smile. Phil could

....

edged came quietly
scanned looked around

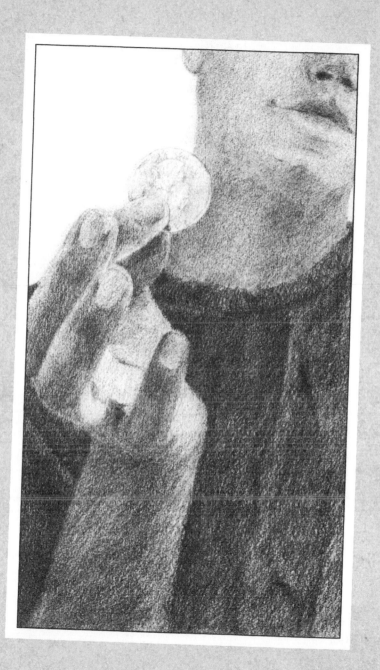

see that. It was a smile that said "**Gotcha.**"

Phil shook his head and **felt himself starting to blush**. "No, that's okay. I don't want the ice cream anyway."

"You sure?" asked Daniel, his smile getting bigger. "What's the matter? It's a gift—I'm just being *kind.*"

Phil put the ice-cream sandwich back in the freezer. He took his tray and walked stiffly to a table where some of his friends were sitting. He **took a seat** facing the wall and began to eat, tearing off big mouthfuls of soft grilled cheese, chewing without tasting. He didn't talk and he didn't look around. When he was done, he dumped his trash, dropped off the tray, and went straight out the side door to the playground.

The cold wind felt good on his burning cheeks. The thing was, Phil saw exactly what Daniel had been doing when he offered him that quarter.

....

Gotcha. Now you are angry about this like I was angry about the jacket.

felt himself starting to blush felt embarrassed; felt his face becoming hot

took a seat sat

Daniel was trying to **get back at him**, to embarrass him with a gift. And it had worked.

Walking beside the fence, kicking a stone ahead of him, Phil kept on thinking. *But Mom giving something to Lucy, that was different, right? Because it's not like Lucy was begging, and it isn't like Mom was trying to make herself feel all rich and grand or make Lucy feel small and poor. Because Mom was just trying to be nice, right? And there's nothing wrong with that. There can't be anything wrong with being kind, can there?*

A burst of laughter came from the other side of the playground, and Phil turned to look. Six black kids, all fourth and fifth graders, all boys. No one was looking his way, but Phil still had the feeling they had been laughing at him. But was it true, or was it just his imagination?

A **gust of wind** made his eyes water, and he zipped his coat up under his chin. And still looking

---

get back at him make Phil feel the same way Daniel felt
gust of wind strong, quick wind

at the black kids, Phil **recognized** one of them, the one with his hands jammed into his pockets and his shoulders **hunched up** against the cold.

He recognized the kid who wasn't wearing a jacket.

....

recognized knew
hunched up lifted

BEFORE YOU MOVE ON...

1. **Character's Motive** Why did Daniel seem so happy to give Phil a quarter in the cafeteria?

2. **Comparisons** Compare how Phil acted on page 34 to how he acted on page 10.

LOOK AHEAD Read pages 38–42 to find out what Phil notices about his neighborhood.

Phil notices there are few African American people in his neighborhood. He thinks he is prejudiced. He tells his mom what happened with Daniel. He asks his mom about Lucy.

Part III

CLOSE TO HOME

Now that he was in sixth grade, Phil walked home from school after basketball practice. It was only six blocks. Sometimes he walked home with a friend or two, sometimes **on his own**. And on the days when it wasn't pouring rain or bitterly cold, he enjoyed it. He liked to take his time getting home, sometimes going a block or two **out of his way** to walk through the little shopping area near his house. If he had some money, he'd stop and buy gum, or maybe a doughnut. And he always liked just looking around, **letting his mind wander along with his eyes**.

....

on his own alone

out of his way away from his street

letting his mind wander along with his eyes thinking while he looked around

But walking home by himself this particular Thursday afternoon, Phil felt like he'd never seen this part of the city before. Everywhere he looked, he saw white people.

He saw moms driving cars full of kids home from school. White moms and white kids. He saw the neat **row houses** with tiny front yards where kids had dropped their sleds and little shovels after it snowed last week. Their snowmen and snow forts were half melted now. Phil thought back to spring and summer, when all the little kids had been outside playing. And he tried to remember seeing an African American kid. And he couldn't.

There were larger homes, too. Homes with real driveways and garages and small lawns, some of them surrounded with fancy iron fences. This time of year, in addition to the BEWARE OF DOG signs and the **security system notices**, the fences were decorated with red ribbons and Christmas wreaths.

Phil looked around as he walked, and he tried to think if any black families lived anywhere in his

....

row houses houses that were very close to each other
security system notices signs that said the houses had alarms

39

neighborhood. And he couldn't think of one. Not one family. Not ever.

Phil turned at the corner of Belden Street so he could walk through the shopping area. The small trees that **lined** the street were covered with **blinking lights**, and the storefronts and shop windows were decorated for Christmas. The sidewalks were busier than usual—not crowded, but still there were lots of people. Lots of white people.

Not everyone was white, of course. Phil saw a few Asian people, women mostly, dressed nicely, carrying shopping bags. Plus some Asian kids, junior high school girls. And he saw a high school boy who might have been Hispanic. **It was hard to tell.**

There were some black people in the shopping area, too, but not many. Phil counted as he walked along. He saw four black people—one man and three women. The man was driving a bus, but Phil counted him anyway.

None of the black women on the sidewalks

....

lined were planted along

blinking lights little lights that went on and off

It was hard to tell. He was not sure.

looked like they had been shopping today, no bags or packages. They weren't **browsing**, weren't looking in the store windows. They all looked like they were going somewhere. **Somewhere else.** In fact, two of the black women were waiting at a bus stop, waiting to get on a bus—to go somewhere else. Just like the black kids at school. And Phil thought, *I can tell those women don't live close by. They just don't look like they **belong here**.*

And Phil heard himself. He heard himself thinking that thought. *They just don't look like they belong here.*

Phil stopped so suddenly that a man behind him on the sidewalk almost knocked him down.

"Whoa!" the man said. "Sorry there, young **fella**. You all right?"

Phil nodded **absently** and said, "Yeah, I'm fine."

But it wasn't true. Phil wasn't all right. He stood on the sidewalk, staring as the two women got onto

....

browsing looking in the stores to see if they wanted to buy something

Somewhere else. To a place that was not this shopping area.

belong here *should be here*

fella man

absently without thinking

their bus. And he thought, *This morning, what if Daniel had been a white kid? Would I have grabbed him like that? If he had looked like he belonged in that jacket, would I have said he stole it?*

The bus **pulled** away from the curb, and Phil started walking again. Turning a corner, he looked up and saw his own reflection in a shop window. He saw a white kid. A white kid who looked like he belonged here.

Phil turned away from the window. He began to run, and he didn't stop until he got home.

....

pulled drove

BEFORE YOU MOVE ON...

1. **Conclusions** Reread page 39. Why did Phil feel like he had never seen his own neighborhood before?

2. **Inference** Phil saw his reflection in a shop window. Why did he feel he looked like he belonged in his neighborhood?

LOOK AHEAD What does Phil begin to think about himself? Read pages 43–48 to find out.

When his mom opened the front door at five fifteen, Phil was waiting for her.

"How come you never told me I was prejudiced?"

His mom set a grocery bag on the floor and looked at him. "What? What are you talking about?"

"I'm prejudiced. I am, and you never told me."

"Who says you're prejudiced? Somebody call you that?"

"No, but it's true. I know what it means because we learned about it on Martin Luther King Day. It means you don't like black people."

"All right," his mom said, "just **hold it right there**. Let me get my coat off, then come into the kitchen with me and tell me **what this is all about**."

So as his mom started making dinner Phil sat on a stool at the tall counter and told her what had happened at school. When he got to the part in the principal's office when Daniel threw the jacket down, she **clucked her tongue** and said, "Poor dear—he must have felt so embarrassed."

Then Phil told about walking home. "No black

....

hold it right there wait
what this is all about why you are saying you are prejudiced
clucked her tongue made a sound that meant she felt sad

people live around here, Mom. None. And when I saw these black ladies in front of the bakery, like, waiting for a bus, I said to myself, 'They don't belong here'—just like that. Like *I* belong here because I'm white, and *they* don't because they're black. So that's prejudiced, right? I'm prejudiced, and I didn't even know it."

Standing at the stove, his mom said, "But you're not prejudiced, honey. Stop saying that."

Phil shook his head. "But it's true. I think I am."

"Well, **take it from me**, you're not. It's all in your imagination. You're not prejudiced. You're just a kid, and you're a good kid, too. You had this problem with another boy, and the boy **happens to be** black. That's all. And we live in a part of town where it's mostly white people. Tell me this, did you choose to live here?"

"No."

"See? **You've got nothing to do with it.** Did you even choose to be white? Is that your fault?"

"Well, no."

"Exactly. Now, stop worrying about this and set

---

take it from me believe me

happens to be is

You've got nothing to do with it. It is not anything that you did.

the table. But first go wash your hands, and knock on Juliana's door and tell her to come help me **get the supper on**."

Phil started to climb off the stool, and then stopped. "How come you gave Lucy that jacket?"

"Because it's a perfectly good jacket, and Jimmy didn't want it, and I knew Lucy had a grandson who **might fit it**."

"You knew Lucy had a grandson?"

"Sure, I knew."

"And you didn't give it to her because she's poor and black?"

"No, of course not. Your old blue **blazer** from fourth grade? I just gave that to Mickey Colter's mom, and you know they're not poor, and they're not black, either. When you have something nice to share, you share. Besides, Lucy's my friend."

Phil nodded. "Only, not really your friend, right?"

His mom looked at him **sternly**. "What's that supposed to mean?"

---

get the supper on serve the dinner

might fit it could wear it; was the right size for it

blazer suit jacket

sternly seriously

"I mean, if she's really a friend, then, like, you'd go to the movies with her sometimes, right? Or **have her over** for dinner with her family, or maybe go bowling, like with you and Mrs. Donato?"

His mom tilted her head, choosing her words carefully. "Well . . . right. Lucy's not that kind of a friend, not really a close friend. More like someone you know at work."

"So . . . have you ever had a friend who's black— I mean, a close friend?"

"No, not really."

"How come?"

"It just never happened, that's all."

"Maybe it's because you're prejudiced, too, like . . . like me, and you didn't know it. Like me."

"For the last time, Philip, you are *not* prejudiced. Now, just forget about it and go get your sister to come down here. Right now."

Phil knew **that tone of voice**. It meant "**end of discussion**." He got off the stool and was going out the doorway when his mom said, "And Philip, let's

....

have her over ask her to come to our house

that tone of voice what his mom meant when her voice sounded like that

end of discussion do not talk about it again

not talk about this to your dad."

He turned around and looked at her. "Why?"

"Because it'll just upset him, that's all."

"How come?"

"Because I know your father, and it just will, that's all."

Phil shrugged, then turned and **headed for** the stairway.

He didn't ask "How come?" again. He didn't have to.

He was **pretty** sure he knew why his dad would get upset. There was only one answer Phil could think of: *It has to be because Dad is . . . prejudiced— like me.*

....

headed for walked to

pretty almost

BEFORE YOU MOVE ON...

1. **Character's Point of View** Phil thought he was prejudiced. Why?

2. **Character** Reread pages 43–45. How did Phil's mother react to him? What does this show about her?

LOOK AHEAD Will Phil forget about his fight with Daniel? Read pages 49–53 to find out.

Phil sees the jacket in the principal's office.
He thinks about it all day. Finally, he takes
the jacket from the office.

Part IV

FORGET ABOUT IT

Friday morning was cold, **complete with rain and sleet driven by a stiff west wind**. It was the kind of day when Phil rode the school bus. He didn't ride that often, so he was **looking forward to** it.

Climbing the steps, he smiled at the driver. Then he turned and looked for a seat. He saw one near the back, but scanning the bus, he also saw something else. *This whole bus is white kids. Only white kids! No, 'cause there's Julie Chin, and she's not white. But she's not black. No black kids on my bus, not one.*

....

complete with rain and sleet driven by a stiff west wind
rainy, icy, and windy

looking forward to excited about

This whole bus is white kids. *There are only white kids on this bus.*

Phil **had done pretty well** until he got on the bus. Because he'd been trying to forget about everything that had happened on Thursday. That's what his mom had said he should do. She'd said, "Forget about it." So he'd tried. Because during dinner and most of Thursday night it was all he could think about, about his being white. And about feeling prejudiced. But he hadn't said anything more about it, because his mom had said he shouldn't. Especially not to his dad. "Forget about it."

But looking around, Phil tried to imagine what it would be like for Daniel if he were on this bus right now. Would that make Daniel feel **weird**? *Or how about if I was on Daniel's bus right now? What would* that *be like?*

Because Phil knew that Daniel's bus was **practically** all black kids. And the part of town where Daniel's bus was coming from, it had to be almost the opposite from his, right? Like, only black families and no white families. And Phil thought,

....

had done pretty well was not thinking about his problems
weird uncomfortable
practically almost

*You can **figure out** a lot just from looking around a bus.*

Phil would have kept thinking about it, but his friend Lee poked him on the shoulder and said, "Hey, Phil, **what'd** you get on that social studies test?"

So for the rest of the short ride to school Phil and Lee talked about how boring social studies was and how stupid it was to have to learn about Ancient Egypt. Except for the Pyramids. Plus mummies and treasure and **junk** like that. That part was okay.

Phil was glad to keep talking. For about five minutes it helped him forget about all that other stuff. But after getting off the bus, he walked up the front steps and into the school, then turned left to go to his locker. And as he passed the big windows of the office he glanced to his right. And he saw

....

figure out *learn, understand*

what'd *what did*

junk *other things*

something that **made everything come crashing back into his head**—the jacket, hanging there on the coatrack outside Mrs. Cormier's office. Jimmy's jacket. Then he thought, *No, it's Daniel's jacket.*

....

made everything come crashing back into his head made him think about Daniel and the jacket again

BEFORE YOU MOVE ON...

1. **Inference** Reread page 50. Why did Phil think about Daniel again when he got on the bus?

2. **Cause and Effect** Why was Phil so surprised to see the jacket on the coatrack outside Mrs. Cormier's office?

LOOK AHEAD Read to page 61 to find out why Phil brings his lunch to school.

There was no way Phil could **avoid going past** the office during his day. Hurrying to math for first period, as he came to the big windows he looked down at the floor and counted ten footsteps before he looked up again.

On his way back to art class he pretended the office wasn't there. He turned his head to the left and **admired** the plaques and posters on the opposite wall.

Going to the library for third-period reading, he studied the pattern on the shirt of the kid in front of him in line. And after library he **cut** through the auditorium. He told himself it was so he could say hi to Caroline Swanson, who was up on the stage getting ready for music class, but he knew it wasn't true. He went that way so he wouldn't have to walk past the office again.

Then on his way to lunch Phil couldn't **help himself**. He sneaked a look through the office window. The jacket was still there.

Phil had brought a bag lunch. He'd done it on

....

avoid going past not pass
admired looked at
cut walked
help himself stop himself

purpose so he could just walk into the cafeteria and go right to his table and sit down and eat. He didn't want to stand around in the lunch line, **just in case**. *Because Daniel might be looking for me, like he'll maybe try to embarrass me again. And maybe Daniel talked to all his friends about me. Like maybe they're **gonna gang up on me** out on the playground. Or maybe Daniel cut out my picture from the yearbook and put it on the Internet, and now everybody in the world knows I'm prejudiced! Except my mom.*

But of course nothing happened at lunch or at recess. Even though he **kept a sharp lookout**, Phil didn't spot Daniel once. That made him curious, so after recess he went to his social studies classroom a few minutes early.

He walked to the front of the room, and Mr. Linton looked up from the book he was reading, **his face lifting into a smile** when he saw Phil. "How's it going, Phil?"

"Okay." Phil smiled and put his hands in his pockets, trying to look casual. Mr. Linton waited

---

just in case because he might see Daniel or his friends
gonna gang up on me going to fight me
kept a sharp lookout looked closely
his face lifting into a smile smiling

a second or two to see if Phil had anything else to say, then nodded and turned back to his book.

Mr. Linton's desk was messy, but Phil knew what he was looking for. And when he saw it, he knew why he hadn't seen Daniel at lunch or recess. Daniel was on the **absent list**.

Class began, but Phil didn't hear much of what Mr. Linton was saying. He was remembering Daniel out on the playground yesterday, out in the freezing cold—without a jacket. *Jeez! He's probably sick. He's probably **got something terrible** 'cause it was so cold. Like really, really sick. Or he's at the hospital or something. And if the doctor says "How come you're so sick?" what's he gonna say? He's gonna say it's all because of me! And what if he . . . what if he dies? Oh, my God! They're gonna put me in prison! I'm a killer!*

Phil knew **his imagination was running away with him**. But still, he decided he had to do something.

---

absent list list of kids who were not at school that day

got something terrible very sick

his imagination was running away with him he was thinking many things that would not happen

• • •

About ten minutes before the last bell of the day **Phil got permission from his English teacher to** go to the office. He said there might be a message there from his mom. Which was true. Because there *might* be one. Except Phil knew there wasn't.

He stopped at his locker first and got his backpack, along with his math book and his social studies homework. He also grabbed his gym bag, but he took out his shoes and shirt and shorts and left them in the locker.

Phil hurried to the office. **His timing was perfect.** It was that quiet moment right before the **end-of-day craziness** begins. The principal was already out in front of the school getting ready **for the bus loading**. It was only Phil and Mrs. Donne in the office. Which was what Phil wanted.

....

Phil got permission from his English teacher to Phil asked his English teacher to let him

His timing was perfect. He came to the office at the best time.

end-of-day craziness busy time at the end of the day

for the bus loading to help kids get on the bus

Stepping toward one end of the long counter, he said, "Can I buy a pencil? I really need one for math 'cause Mrs. Kinnon doesn't let us use pens."

Mrs. Donne sighed and said, "All right. **Hang on** while I get one out for you."

She got up slowly from her desk and walked to the storeroom at the rear of the office. Which was just what Phil knew she would do, because that's where the school store supplies were kept. And when she went into the storeroom, Phil **took a quick step** to the left, grabbed the jacket off the coatrack, bent down below the counter, and stuffed it into his unzipped gym bag. When he **straightened** up, Mrs. Donne was coming back through the storeroom door. Phil's face was flushed, but he smiled as best he could, and when she laid the pencil on the counter, he handed her fifteen

....

Hang on Wait
took a quick step walked quickly
straightened stood

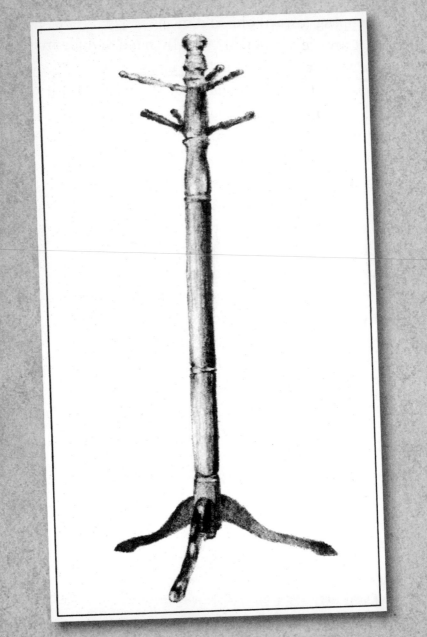

cents, gulped, and said, "Thanks."

"You're welcome. Have a good weekend, dear."

"You, too."

Phil left the office, and as he walked down the stairs and out the door to get on bus number seven, he carefully closed the long zipper on his gym bag.

....

"You, too." "I hope you have a good weekend, too."

BEFORE YOU MOVE ON...

1. **Conflict** Phil brought his lunch because he was scared to stand in the lunch line. What did he think could happen?

2. **Sequence** Reread pages 58–61. Phil left Mr. Linton's class and went to the principal's office. What did he do next?

LOOK AHEAD Read pages 62–67 to find out what Phil talks about with his dad.

Phil's dad thinks that black athletes get too much attention. He barely says hi to Lucy. Is Phil's dad prejudiced? Phil decides to go visit Daniel.

Part V

SOMETHING IN
THE TONE

Phil usually **slept in** on Saturday morning, so his dad was surprised to see him in the kitchen a little before nine.

"Early basketball practice today?"

"Nope. Just couldn't sleep." Phil **gave a big yawn**.

"Couple'a eggs sound good?"

"Sure."

Phil grabbed a clean glass from the dishwasher,

---

slept in woke up late

gave a big yawn yawned

"Couple'a eggs sound good?" "Do you want to eat two eggs for breakfast?"

got out the orange juice, poured himself a glass, and sat down.

His dad liked to cook, and Phil watched as he cracked both eggs, one-handed, against the side of the frying pan. As they started to sizzle in the butter his dad said, "So, how's the team look this year?"

"Team looks good. First game's next week against Regina."

"You gonna **start**?" asked his dad, one eyebrow cocked.

Phil shook his head. "I don't think so. There's another guy who's taller than I am, and he's a really good shooter, too. I'm gonna get to play, but I think the coach'll start him at center instead of me."

"This other center—black kid?"

Phil heard something in the **tone of** the question. "Yeah—Dennis Hardy."

"**Figures**," his dad said, flipping first one egg then the other.

Definitely something in that tone.

....

start be one of the players who will play at the beginning of the game

tone of way his father asked

Figures That is what I thought

Phil said, "What d'you mean?"

His dad shrugged. "I mean, find me a team anywhere in the whole country that's not mostly blacks, that's all. And now even golf. Prob'ly bowling next. Be nice if some other folks **got some game**, too, that's all." He slid the cooked eggs onto a plate, dropped on two pieces of toast, put it down in front of Phil, and said, **"Breakfast of champions. Eat up."** Then he sat down across the table, picked up his coffee mug, and turned to a **fresh** page of the sports section.

Phil ate a bite of eggs and then drank some of his juice. "Dad?"

"Hmm?"

"Don't you think it's great to watch a game when guys like Shaq and Hardaway and Ewing play? I mean, they're great players, right? And Jordan? He's *the* best, right?"

His dad shrugged. "Sure. Don't **get me wrong**. It's fine that those guys are so great. Great is great. But see what I mean? When you think about great,

....

got some game could play

"Breakfast of champions. Eat up." "This is a good breakfast. Eat it."

fresh new

get me wrong misunderstand me

do you remember Bob Cousy or Larry Bird or Bill Walton? No, you remember Wilt Chamberlain and Magic Johnson. And players like Ainge and Stockton? Forget about it. **These days it's all about the black guys.** So **don't get me started**."

There was a knock at the kitchen door, and Phil looked at the clock. Nine. That was Lucy. He got up and opened the door for her. "Hi, Lucy."

She smiled and said, "Well, Philip! This is a surprise—**you're up bright and early** this morning."

"Uh-huh."

Then Lucy saw his dad at the table. Phil watched her. Lucy seemed to pause a second, adjusting her face and her voice. Then she said, "Morning, Mr. Morelli."

Phil watched, and his dad didn't look up from the newspaper. "Hi," he said. And again Phil could hear something in the tone of his dad's voice. And Phil knew that Lucy could hear it, too.

Walking out of the kitchen, Phil passed Jimmy

These days it's all about the black guys. At this time, there are too many black players and not enough white players.

don't get me started I don't want to talk about it

you're up bright and early you woke up very early

in the family room, **glued to the TV, flipping from cartoon to cartoon**. But Phil hardly noticed. He was thinking.

All his life Lucy had called him Philip, and she had called his brother Jimmy, and his sister Juliana. And for as long as he could remember, Lucy had called his mom June, because that was her name—June. Because, like his mom had said, Lucy was a friend.

But Phil couldn't remember Lucy ever using his dad's first name. She always called him Mr. Morelli. Never Nick. Always Mr. Morelli. And for the first time in his life Phil understood why.

....

glued to the TV, flipping from cartoon to cartoon watching the television, changing the channels

BEFORE YOU MOVE ON...

1. **Generalization** Phil talked with his dad about sports. What did Phil's dad think about African American players in sports?

2. **Conclusions** Reread pages 66–67. What did Phil think he understood about Lucy and his father?

LOOK AHEAD What does Lucy say about Phil and her grandson? Read pages 68–75 to find out.

●●●

At about eleven fifteen Phil was in his room. His mom had **sent him** there to make sure everything was **picked up** off the floor. So Phil dug some stray socks out from under his bed, picked up the CD cases and books that were spread around on the carpet, and then began stuffing some shoes and a couple of dirty sweatshirts into his closet. For years he and Lucy had had a cleaning day deal: as long as Phil got **the floor clear of obstacles**, she'd leave his closet shut.

Phil pushed the door closed with his shoulder and **flopped** onto his bed to listen to a song. Three minutes later there was a loud knock on his door.

"Come in!" He had to yell to be heard above the music. As Lucy stuck her head into the room Phil hit the stop button on his CD player.

"I've got to work in here, and then I'm going to

---

sent him told him to go
picked up cleaned
the floor clear of obstacles everything off the floor
flopped fell

run the vacuum. **You in or out?**"

"I'll leave in a minute." Phil plugged in his earphones and put them over his ears, but he didn't start the music. He started reading some song lyrics, but he was actually watching Lucy.

She began at his dresser, lifting up each picture, each of his basketball trophies, dusting underneath, and then putting things back. As she worked she hummed a little tune, her hands busy.

Phil pulled off the earphones, **cleared his throat**, and said, "You know, your grandson goes to my school."

Lucy nodded. "I guess I knew that. It's the Curwin School, right?"

"Uh-huh."

Lucy kept working, now dusting the bookshelves above his desk. Phil said, "Did Daniel tell you about what happened on Thursday?"

"Something about his jacket, right? I heard about it, but not from him. I don't think he wants to talk about it."

··

run use

You in or out? Are you going to stay in the room while I clean?

cleared his throat got ready to talk

"Well, it was kind of my fault. I didn't know it was his, so I thought he stole it or something. He got pretty mad about it."

Lucy smiled, nodding again. "He **does have a temper**, that boy. But he **gets over things**. You didn't mean him any harm. Any fool knows that, and he's no fool. Straight A's in all his classes. **Smart as a whip.**"

Lucy had finished dusting, and she stepped into the hallway and pulled the old Electrolux through the doorway.

Phil jumped off his bed. "Here, I'll plug it in."

"Thank you."

Lucy was ready to switch on the vacuum cleaner, but Phil said, "I think I'd like to call him— Daniel. Can you tell me his phone number?"

"Sure can."

And Phil grabbed a pen and a note card off his desk and wrote down the number.

"Thanks, Lucy."

She smiled at him. "You're a good boy, Philip, a

---

does have a temper gets angry easily
gets over things stops feeling angry
Smart as a whip. He is very smart.
"Sure can." "Yes, I can."

nice young man. And so's my Daniel. Now, you **scat out of here** and let me get my work done."

Phil stuffed the note card into his back pocket. He went straight downstairs and into the family room.

As he turned on the computer at the desk against the wall, he felt bad. What he'd just said to Lucy was like what he'd said to his English teacher on Friday, about how there might be a note in the office from his mom. It was almost a lie. Because Phil didn't really intend to give Daniel a call, at least not today. Today Phil had a very different plan.

With a few clicks he **activated the modem**, and it began to **chirp and whine**. Phil knew exactly what he was doing, because he'd been thinking about it all morning. He went to a search engine, clicked on FIND PEOPLE, then clicked on **REVERSE LOOKUP**. He typed in Daniel's phone number, and in two seconds there it was on the screen: 2518 Randall Street. And once he

....

scat out of here leave the room
activated the modem started the Internet
chirp and whine make a noise that showed he was going online
REVERSE LOOKUP find an address using a phone number

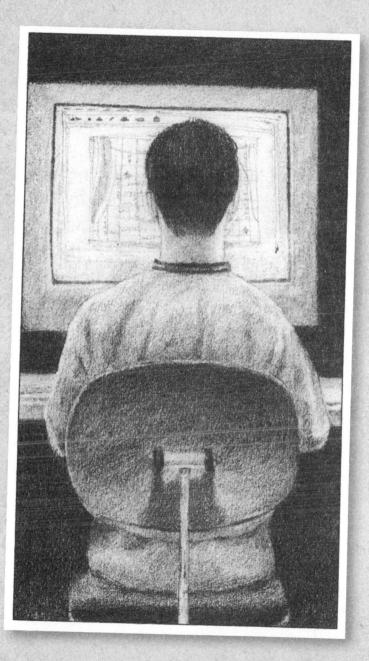

had Daniel's address, after only a few more mouse clicks and a few more key taps, Phil printed out a detailed map that showed exactly how to get from his door to Daniel's.

Studying the map, Phil was surprised. Daniel didn't live that far away, just a little more than two miles. And Phil thought, *Two miles? That's not far at all. I run farther than that during one basketball practice.*

After he **shut down** the computer, Phil went to the front-hall closet and pulled on a stocking cap, his cross trainer Nikes, and a hooded sweatshirt. He stuffed a pair of lightweight gloves into the front pocket of the sweatshirt. Then he leaned down and picked up his gym bag.

In the kitchen Phil peeled a piece of paper from the memo pad by the phone. In large letters he wrote, "Going to run over to Lee's house, maybe play some **B-ball**. Be back later."

As Phil signed his name and put the note under the saltshaker on the kitchen table, he knew he was

....

shut down turned off
B-ball basketball

letting himself get away with another half-truth. Yes, he was actually going to run over to Lee's house. That was the true part. But when he got there, Phil knew he wouldn't stop. He was going to keep on running.

He was going to **take a nice long run**—all the way to 2518 Randall Street.

....

letting himself get away with another half-truth telling part of the truth, but not telling the important part

take a nice long run run a long way

BEFORE YOU MOVE ON...

1. **Character** Why did Lucy say that Phil and her grandson were good boys? What did that show about Lucy?

2. **Conclusions** Reread pages 74–75. Explain how Phil told a "half-truth." Where was he really going?

LOOK AHEAD What is Daniel's neighborhood like? Read pages 76–84 to find out.

Phil runs all the way to Daniel's house. He wonders if Daniel will talk to him. He is surprised to see who answers the door.

Part VI

ROUND-TRIP

The first week of basketball practice had been tough. It had felt like too much running, and Phil had **limped home** every day. But **his legs and his lungs soon learned to obey**, so by the end of the second week Phil **had his running game under control**.

And that's why at eleven fifty-five on a cold, gray Saturday morning, Phil was enjoying himself. He was running. He was ten minutes into a two-mile run and not even breathing hard. The gym

....

limped home walked home slowly because he was tired

his legs and his lungs soon learned to obey he started to feel okay when he went running every day

had his running game under control could run without getting very tired

bag slung across his back was a little annoying, but after Phil pulled the shoulder strap tighter, he hardly noticed it.

As Phil headed west along Coughlin Avenue, the city started to look unfamiliar. He knew the ten square blocks around his own home pretty well, but **this was new territory**. He'd probably **been this way in a car plenty of times**, but that's never the same as being on the sidewalk. Jogging along this way, Phil had time to look at things, time to think.

Phil kept noticing people, kept noticing whether they were white or black or Asian or Hispanic. He couldn't help it. It was as if the city had divided up into colors and races. *And I'm white,* he thought. *I'm a white kid.*

About ten blocks from home Phil began to see more African Americans. About fifteen blocks from home there were a lot more black people than white. And when he was about four blocks from Daniel's street, **the change was complete**. Phil was the only white person on the street.

....

this was new territory he did not know this neighborhood

been this way in a car plenty of times seen this neighborhood many times when he was in a car

the change was complete everything was different

Phil slowed to a walk and looked around. He thought, *Now I'm in Daniel's neighborhood.* He stopped and peered in the front window of a small grocery store. The place was crowded with Saturday shoppers. And Phil counted. *One, two . . . only two white people.*

Walking along, he tried to **get the feel of** the neighborhood. There had been a few places along his run that had not felt good. In one three-block stretch a lot of the buildings had been empty, with broken windows and spray-painted plywood nailed over the doors. And even on this cold day there had been some groups of kids and older teenagers **just standing around**. Now and then there would be a wrecked car at the curb, no tires, hood open, windshield shattered. The guys on the corners had looked at him, but no one had said anything, and Phil had just kept on running.

But this neighborhood **felt fine**. He didn't see any large houses like the ones he passed walking home from school, but the row houses and the two-flats looked friendly and cared for. Then Phil saw

....

get the feel of understand more about
just standing around standing and talking
felt fine seemed safe

a house that looked exactly like his—except his house had a red door instead of a white one. And he thought, *Same house, only different people. And practically the same neighborhood, too!*

Phil was surprised. And when he noticed he was surprised, he thought, *That's because I'm prejudiced, right?*

Because Phil hadn't known what **to expect**. Running along, he had thought back over some books he'd read. Books like *Journey to Jo'burg,* and *The Well.* Books like *Bud, Not Buddy.* These were stories about black people in other countries, or stories about other times and other parts of America, or stories about poor families living in the country. And Phil had seen TV shows like *The Cosby Show* and *The Fresh Prince of Bel-Air,* where black people lived in houses **a lot fancier** than his—even fancier than Grandma Morcone's condo. And Phil could also remember seeing terrible-looking parts of Los Angeles on the TV news.

And Phil thought, *I've known **tons** of black kids all*

....

to expect he would see
a lot fancier more beautiful
tons a lot

my life, and I never knew they could live in houses and neighborhoods just like mine!

And Phil didn't know whether to feel good about that or not, because all these thoughts about black and white were too new.

Also, Phil was less than a block away from Daniel's house now. What had seemed like a terrific idea at school on Friday afternoon suddenly didn't seem so great. He kept seeing the look on Daniel's face as he threw the jacket onto the floor. Phil thought, *What if he **slams the door in my face**?*

Then he was standing in front of a small brick **bungalow**, 2518 Randall Street. And walking up the front steps, Phil stopped. He remembered the smile Daniel had given him in the lunch line, **taunting** him with that quarter, and he thought, *What if he just laughs at me? What then? What if I get mad and punch him or something? Besides, I already said I was sorry once, didn't I? How many times do you have to say sorry to this kid, anyway?*

---

slams the door in my face tells me to go home; will not talk to me

bungalow one-floor house

taunting embarrassing

Phil almost **turned around**, but then he made himself go up the last two steps and push the button of the doorbell. And when the door opened, his mouth dropped open, too. Because it was Lucy who stood there, **a puzzled look on her face**.

"Philip? What in the world? Does your mama know where you are?"

Phil shook his head and then managed to ask, "What are you doing here?"

"Me?" asked Lucy, pulling her chin back and looking down her nose at him. "I live here, that's what I'm doing here. I just drove back from your house, and you are **the last person I expected to have ringing my doorbell** today. Come in here out of the cold."

Standing in the small entryway, Phil stammered, "I . . . I thought this was where Daniel lived."

Lucy nodded. "It is. **Got the whole family under one roof** for a while. His daddy's back in

....

turned around went home

a puzzled look on her face she looked confused

the last person I expected to have ringing my doorbell not someone who I thought would come here

Got the whole family under one roof The whole family is living in the same house

college full-time, and they're saving some rent money, living here until June. So you came to see Daniel, that it?"

Phil nodded.

"Then follow me," and Lucy turned and headed up the staircase that **ran up** the right-hand wall of the living room. Looking around as he followed, Phil thought, *The furniture and that TV, it's as nice as the stuff in our house—I think their TV is bigger.*

....

ran up was near

BEFORE YOU MOVE ON...

1. **Comparisons** Reread pages 78–80. How was Daniel's neighborhood like Phil's neighborhood?

2. **Conclusions** Reread pages 82–84. Why did Lucy answer the door at Daniel's house?

LOOK AHEAD Does Daniel accept Phil's apology? Read pages 85–92 to find out.

Lucy stopped at a door. There was a sign on it, neatly written with red crayon in large block letters: SMALL GIRLS WHO ENTER WILL SUFFER. Lucy pointed at it with her thumb and whispered, "**Daniel's not real fond of** his baby sister right now." Then she knocked and said, "Daniel? **You've got company.**"

Turning to walk away, she whispered, "Remember what I said to you this morning—he's a nice young man. Don't forget that."

Phil took a deep breath and pushed the door open. Daniel was sitting at a computer screen, his back to the door, earphones on. Phil recognized the game on the screen—*Warcraft*—and Daniel was in the middle of a battle. He hadn't heard Lucy knock on his door.

Phil didn't know what to do. He **glanced around, taking in the room**. There were CD cases on the floor, and some books and papers were spread out across the table next to the computer. The bed wasn't made, and a pair of jeans and

....

Daniel's not real fond of Daniel does not like

You've got company. Someone is here to see you.

glanced around, taking in the room looked around at everything in the room

a red T-shirt were sticking out of a half-open
dresser drawer. There was a big poster on the wall,
probably a band. Five guys with crazy hats and lots
of gold chains—five black guys. A small bookcase
next to the bed was too full, and someone had
started stacking paperbacks on top of it.

Phil thought, *Can't **back down** now,* and he
took three steps forward and tapped Daniel on the
shoulder.

Daniel shook his head, eyes still on the screen.
"Can't stop. Got to get to a village so I can save the
game. I'll eat later."

Phil tapped again. "Hey—it's me."

Daniel swung his chair around. He saw Phil,
and **his eyes jerked wide**. He yanked off the
headphones. "What?! What . . . how . . . how did you
get here?" He jumped up and **faced Phil squarely**.

Phil tried to smile. "I walked . . . I mean, I ran.
From my house. It's not that far. I . . . I brought
you this." Phil unzipped his bag and pulled out the
jacket.

....

back down walk away
his eyes jerked wide he looked very surprised
faced Phil squarely looked at Phil

Small soldiers on the computer screen began dying in large numbers, but Daniel wasn't watching. He cocked his head to one side and said, "How come?"

"Because it's yours. And it's cold outside."

Daniel narrowed his eyes and looked up into Phil's face. "What, you think I don't have other stuff to wear? **That it?** You gonna help me 'cause you think I'm so poor?"

Phil felt his face turn red. **That very thought had run through his head** earlier this morning. But it wasn't true. He knew that now. Daniel wasn't anywhere near poor. So he said, "I brought it because it's a good jacket and . . . and it's stupid to let something go to waste, that's all."

"You callin' me stupid?"

Phil felt the anger rising in his chest, but he choked it back. "No. Look, I'm sorry I grabbed you, okay? So just take the jacket."

"So I just take the jacket, and then **you're done with your good deed for the day**, right?"

....

That it? Is that what you think?

That very thought had run through his head Daniel was right. Phil had thought that Daniel was poor

you're done with your good deed for the day you can feel that you did a good thing today

With **his nostrils flared and his lips trembling with anger**, Phil almost spit the words: "Take it, don't take it, wear it, don't wear it—I don't care! There!" He threw the jacket at Daniel's feet. "I'm outta here."

Phil was down the stairs and at the front door before Daniel caught up to him.

"Hey!"

Phil swung around, his head low, shoulders hunched, fists ready.

Daniel had the jacket under one arm, and he held up his other hand, palm out. "Hey . . . it's okay. I shouldn't have **messed with** you."

Phil put his hands down, still breathing hard.

Daniel said, "You **coming here took some guts**." He smiled. "And how'd you get through Carter Terrace? All those boarded-up buildings? Not a nice place to walk."

Phil smiled. "Like I said, I didn't walk. I ran."

Nodding, Daniel said, "I would, too."

A swinging door opened behind Daniel, and

----

his nostrils flared and his lips trembling with anger an angry look on his face

messed with become mad at

coming here took some guts were brave to come here

Lucy stuck her head out and said, "Lunchtime, boys. Daniel, you show Philip where to wash his hands."

Phil said, "I . . . **I've got to get to get going.**"

Lucy shook her head. "No you don't, because I just talked to your mother, and I told her I'll be driving you home after you eat, and **that's that**. Daniel, you show Philip where to wash his hands."

Lucy **did most of the talking** during lunch, which was fine with Phil. His long run had made him hungry. The bread was fresh, the peanut butter was smooth, the sliced apples were crunchy, and once Daniel started dipping his Oreo cookies in his milk, Phil did, too. Everything tasted great, and Phil thought, *Just like lunch at home. Same stuff.* And Phil didn't want to feel surprised about that, but he was. He had thought everything would be so different here. And it wasn't. It just wasn't.

Daniel rode along in the car when Lucy drove Phil home after lunch, the two boys buckled into the backseat of the little Honda. When they drove by the **derelict** buildings, Daniel said, "Better to

....

I've got to get going. I should go home.
that's that that is what is going to happen
did most of the talking talked more than Phil or Daniel
derelict empty, falling apart

ride right past this place."

And Phil nodded. "Yeah."

Other than that, they didn't talk. But there was no **strain in the silence** because neither boy was waiting for anything.

Daniel wasn't looking for more words. Phil had already said he was sorry. Twice. Because sometimes sorry has to be said twice. Sometimes even more.

And Phil wasn't waiting for Daniel to say thanks. Because it wasn't needed. It was understood.

When Phil got out of the car in front of his house, Lucy leaned over so she could look up into his face. "I've got things all settled with your mom. She wasn't happy about you running that far from home, but I **got her calmed down**."

Phil made a sheepish face and said, "Thanks, Lucy. I **owe you one**." Then he looked at Daniel and smiled. "See ya round."

....

strain in the silence problem that they were not talking

got her calmed down talked to her so she is not angry

owe you one must do something nice for you because you helped me

And Daniel nodded and said, "Later."

Phil started to shut the door, but then he leaned down, pointed at Daniel, and said, "Been meaning to tell you—that's a nice jacket."

Daniel grinned. "Yeah, it's okay. Used to belong to this kid I know. He's a good guy."

Phil said, "Yeah?"

Daniel nodded. "Yeah, **he's all right**."

Phil watched the little car from his front walk until it went around the corner. Then he turned and went up the porch steps, two at a time.

....

he's all right I like him

BEFORE YOU MOVE ON...

1. **Inference** Reread page 87. Why do you think Daniel did not accept Phil's apology?

2. **Character** Phil and Daniel did not talk much on the ride home. Why were they quiet? Are they still angry?